The Soldier who gave orders

© Copyright 1994 by Kevin Mayhew Ltd.

KEVIN MAYHEW LTD
Rattlesden Bury St Edmunds
Suffolk England
IP30 0SZ

OPENBOOK PUBLISHERS
205 Halifax Street
Adelaide
SA 5000
Australia

ISBN 0 86209 427 5

Printed in Great Britain

The Soldier who gave orders

Retold from Scripture by Susan Sayers
and illustrated by Arthur Baker

Kevin Mayhew

'Good morning, sir! Here are your sandals and washing water,' said Festin, hoping he hadn't spilt too much. Quentus yawned and smiled. 'Ah, thank you, Festin,' he said, 'you are learning to be a good servant. Now run along and have your breakfast.'

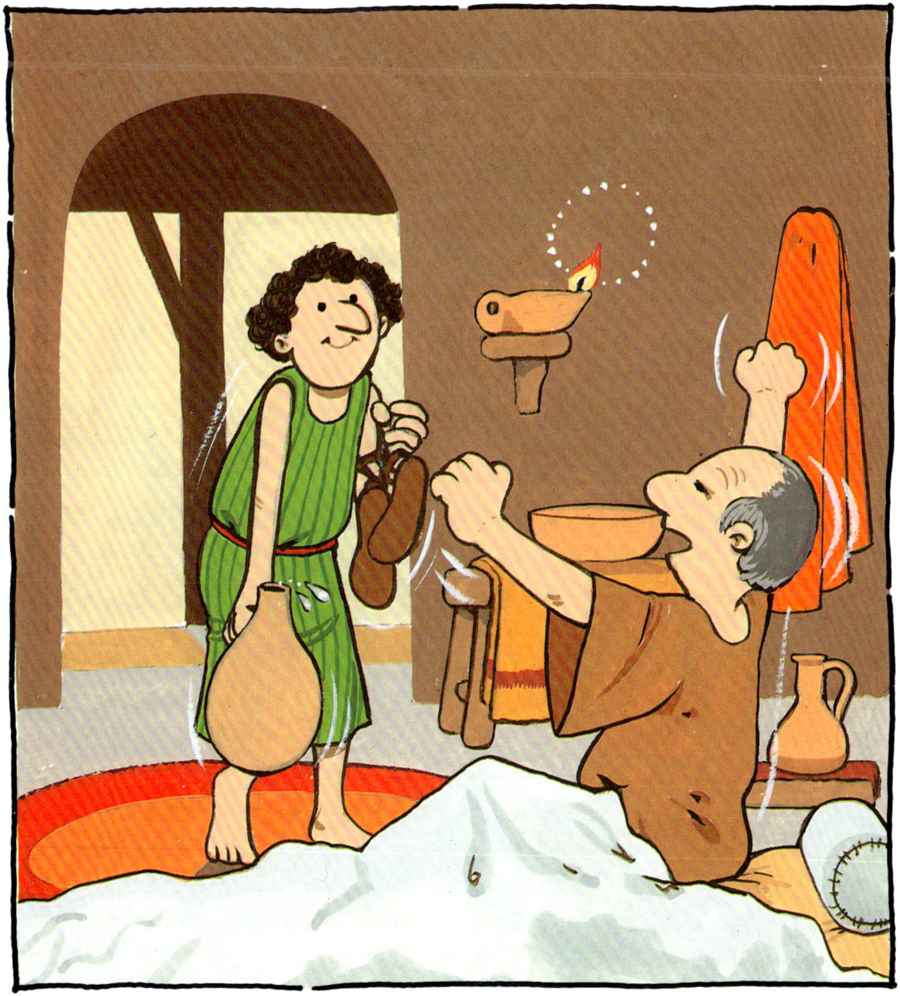

Festin trotted off happily. He liked working for his new master. Quentus was strict, but very kind. In his soldier's uniform he looked really important, because he was a centurion, in charge of a hundred men. But in bed he just looked a bit like Festin's dad – comfortable and whiskery.

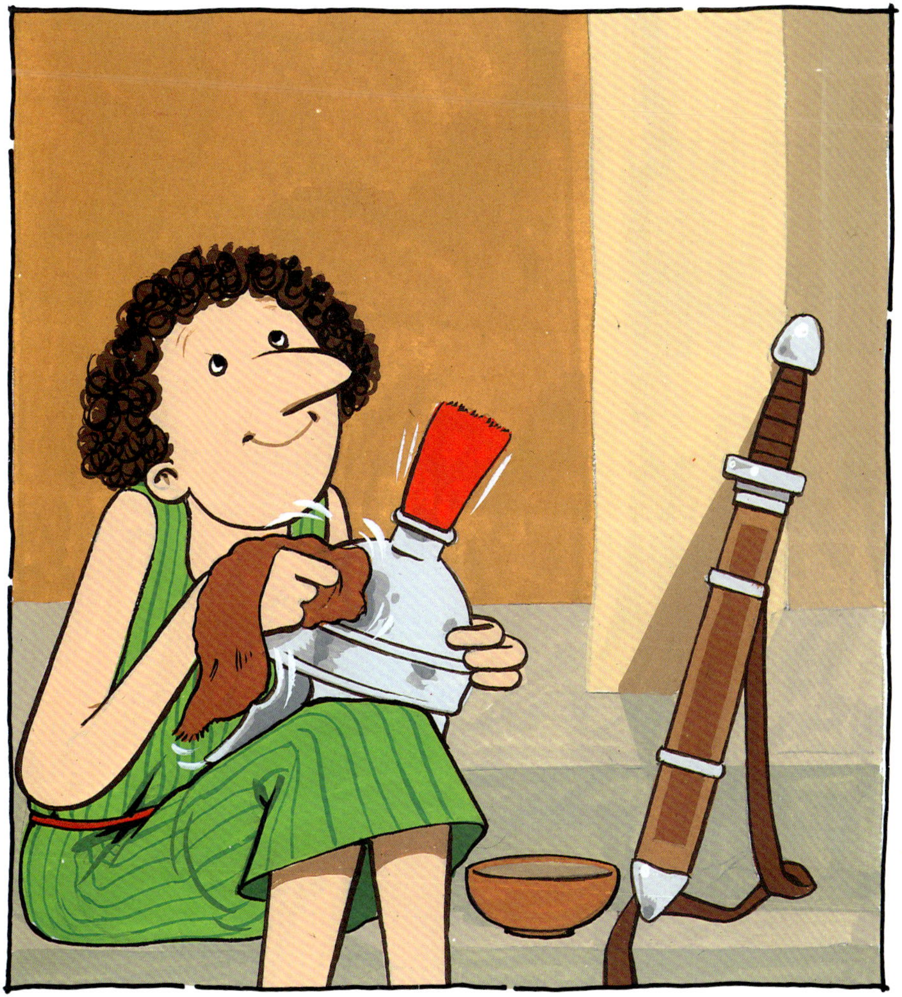

That morning they set off through their town, Capernaum. Festin's job was to walk behind Quentus, carrying things or running messages. Everyone bowed or waved to Quentus as they marched (and scampered) along.

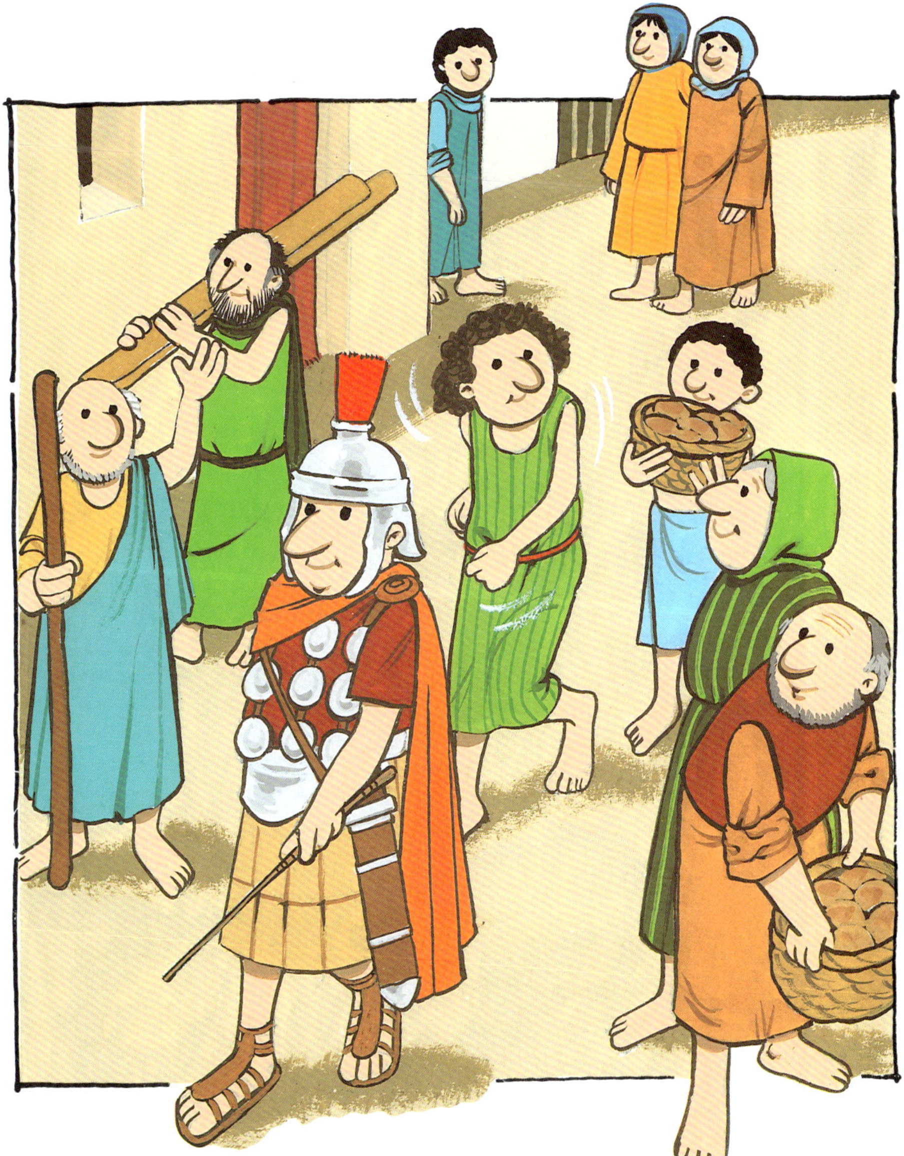

First stop was the synagogue. 'Any problems?' asked Quentus. 'Just a small leak, sir,' said the builder. 'Ezra could fix it for us.' 'Right, Festin,' ordered Quentus, 'run and fetch Ezra. Tell him to come straight away.'

Festin was off like a javelin. 'Yes, sir!' he shouted. And sure enough, that leak was fixed in no time.

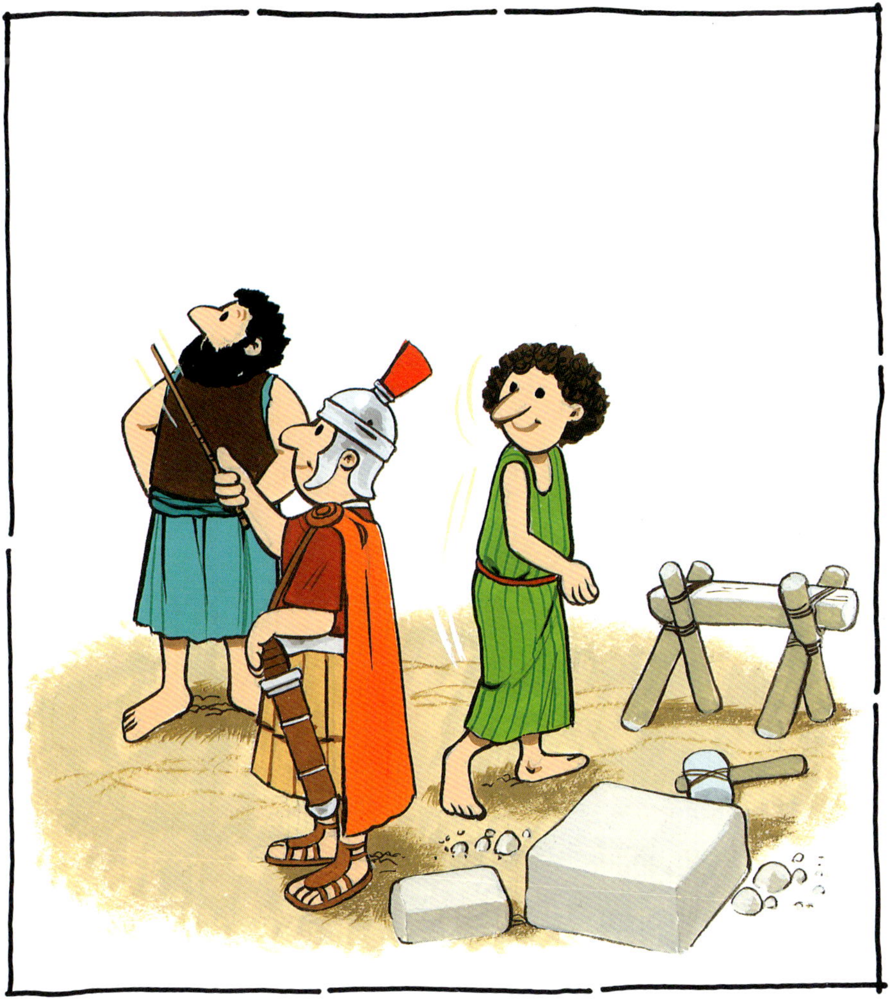

Next they met a family dancing in the street. One woman danced up to Quentus. 'Excuse me, sir,' she gasped, 'but my daughter has just had a baby son and we're SO happy.' 'Well, congratulations!' beamed Quentus. 'May I join in?' 'Of course,' said everyone. So Festin and Quentus danced as well.

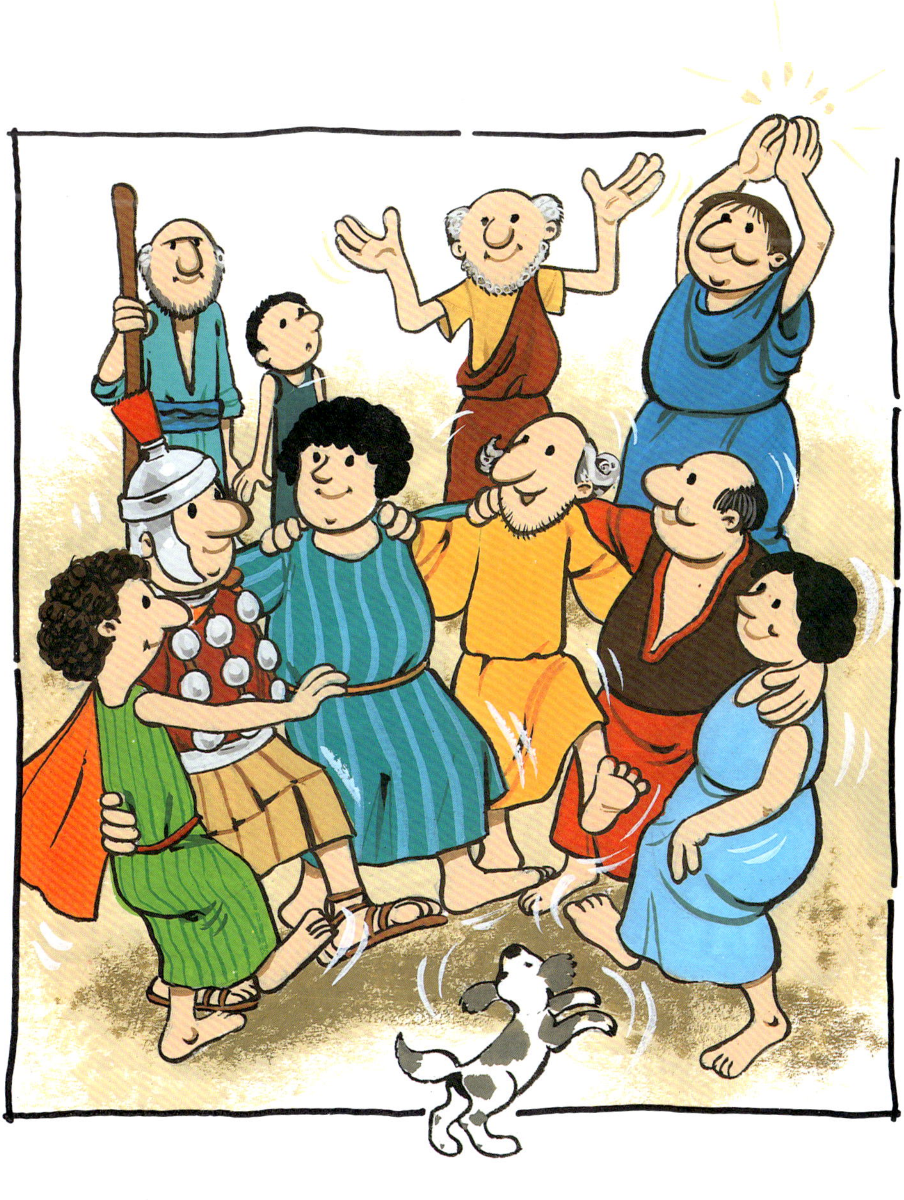

Then the soldiers had to be inspected. Quentus barked orders, and they all obeyed.

'Atten . . . TION!'

'Quick . . . MARCH!'

'About . . . TURN!'

Festin would have liked to join in.

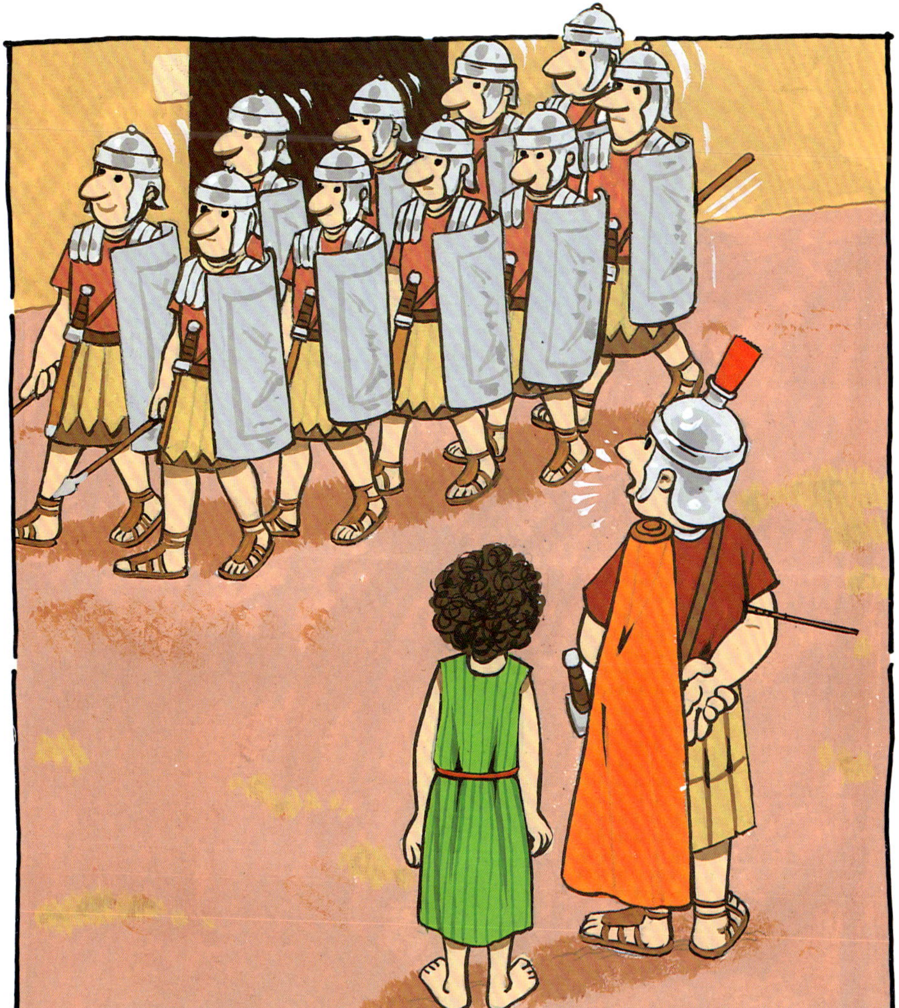

One day Festin woke up in awful pain. He felt really ill, and couldn't move at all. Quentus came to see him. He bathed his head and made him more comfortable. 'Poor young Festin,' he said, 'we must get you well again.'

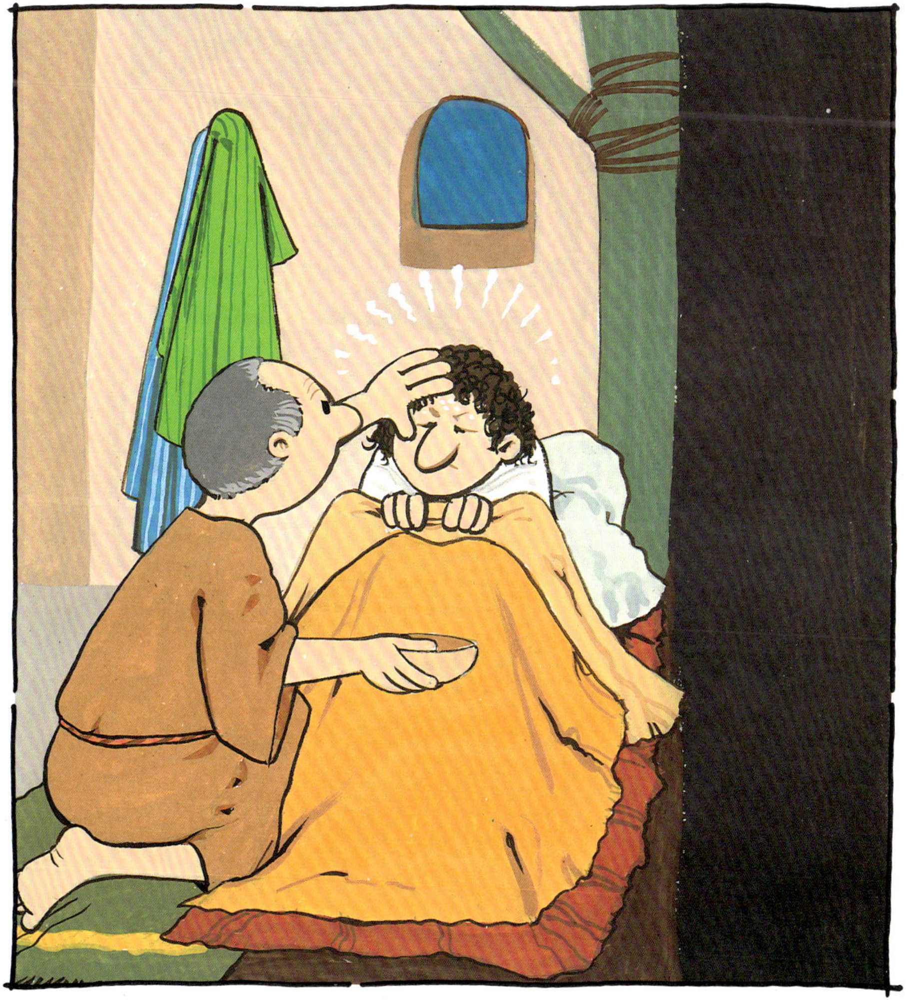

But Festin didn't get better. He got
worse. Quentus paced up and
down looking sad.

Then he had an idea. A man called
Jesus was visiting Capernaum
that day, and he was good at
making people well. Quentus saw
him in the distance and marched
up to him.

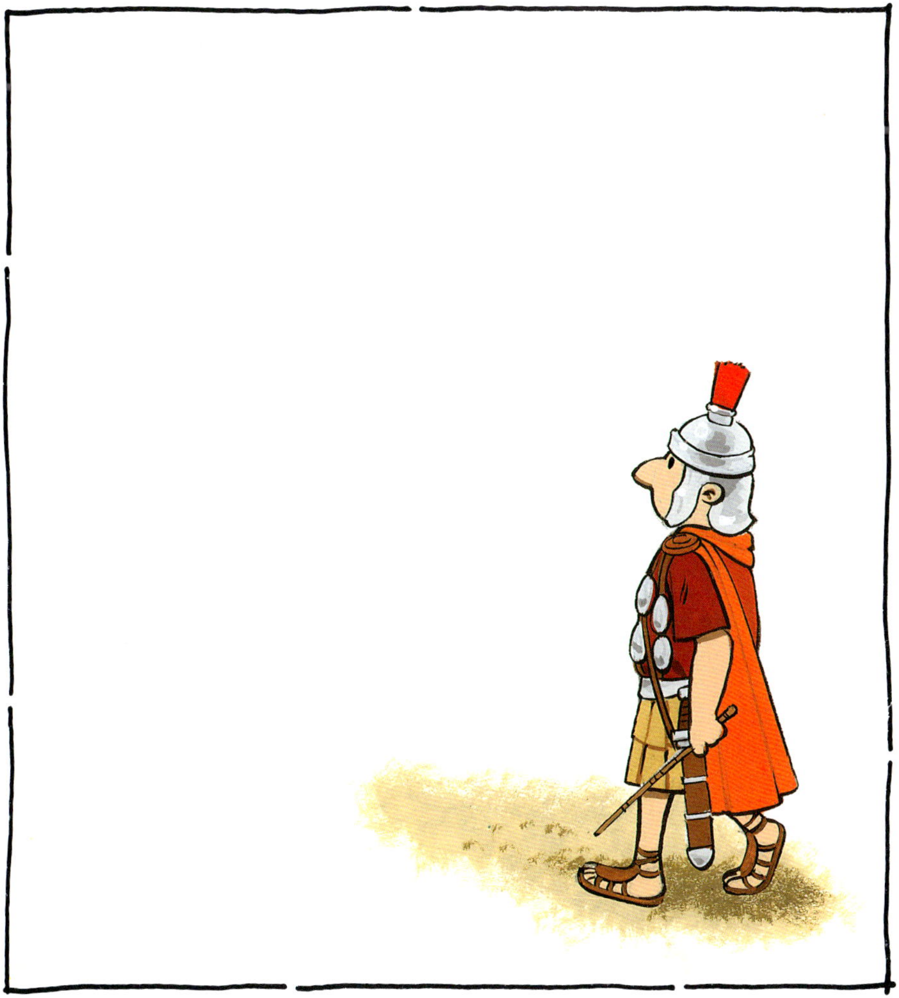

'Sorry to bother you, sir,' he said to Jesus, 'but my young servant can't move and is in terrible pain.'
'Then I will heal him,' said Jesus.
The people crowded round. 'Yes, do help him, Jesus,' they begged. 'This centurion is such a good man . . . he even built our synagogue!' The centurion went quite pink and looked hard at his toes.

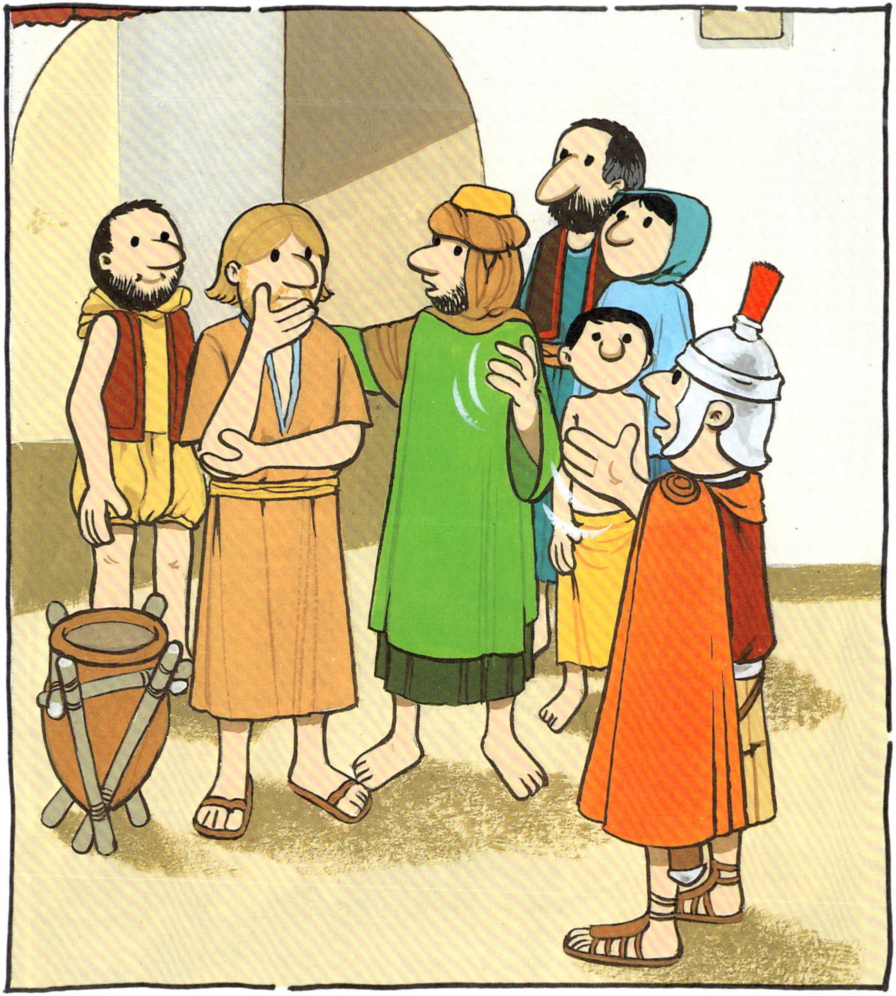

Then he cleared his throat. 'Hmm hmm. Sir, I'm a soldier,' he began, 'so I'm used to giving orders. I tell this man "Come!" and he comes; I tell that man "Go!" and he goes.

'Well, you have much more power than I have. I'm not important enough to have you visit my house, but if you just give the order, sir, I know my servant will be healed.'

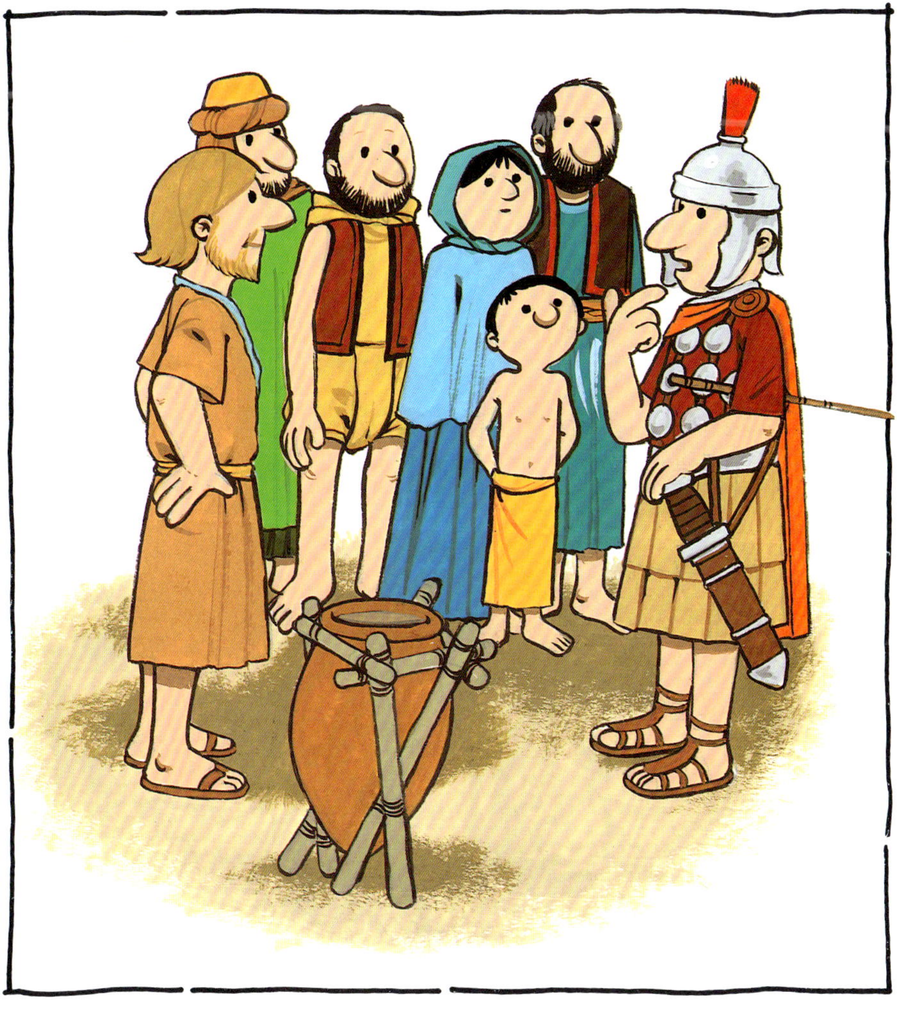

Jesus looked at him in amazement and delight. 'Do you know,' he said at last, 'I have never met anyone who trusts me so much, anywhere before – not even in Israel!'

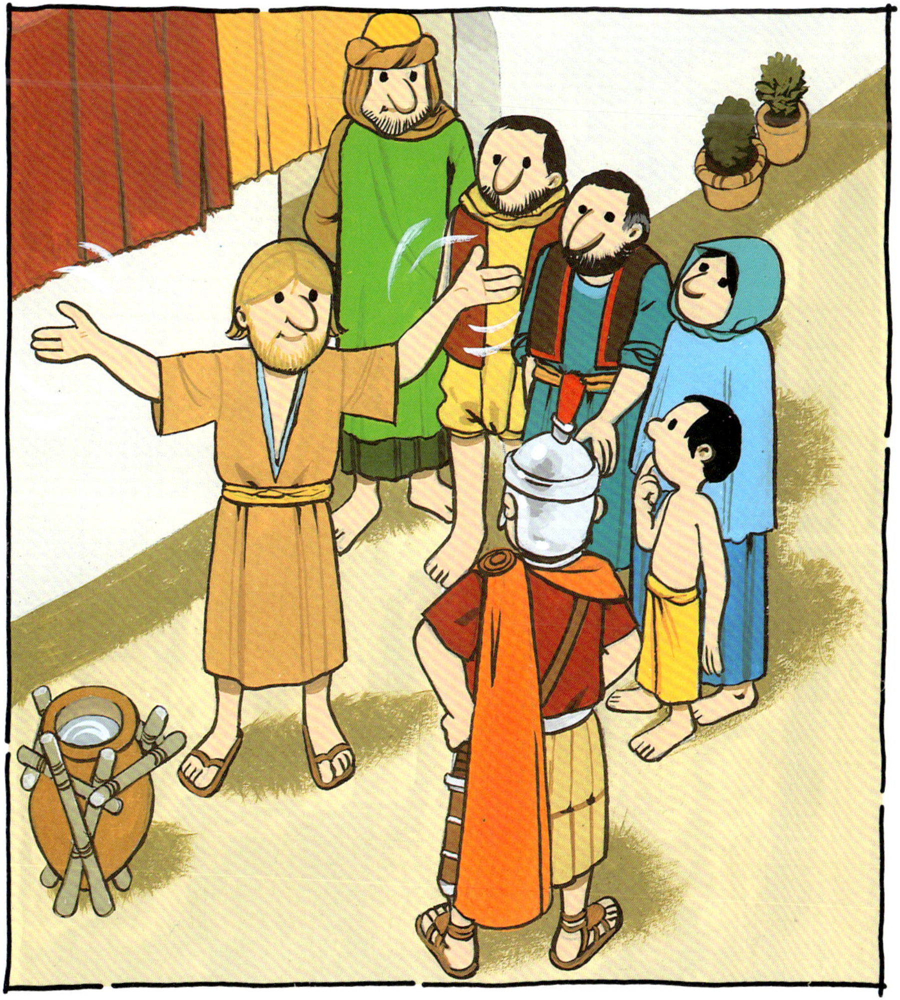

Then Jesus turned to Quentus. 'You can go home now. Let your servant be healed, just as you believed he would be.'

Quentus bowed smartly, thanked Jesus, and marched home. His march soon turned into a gallop – he couldn't wait to see Festin.

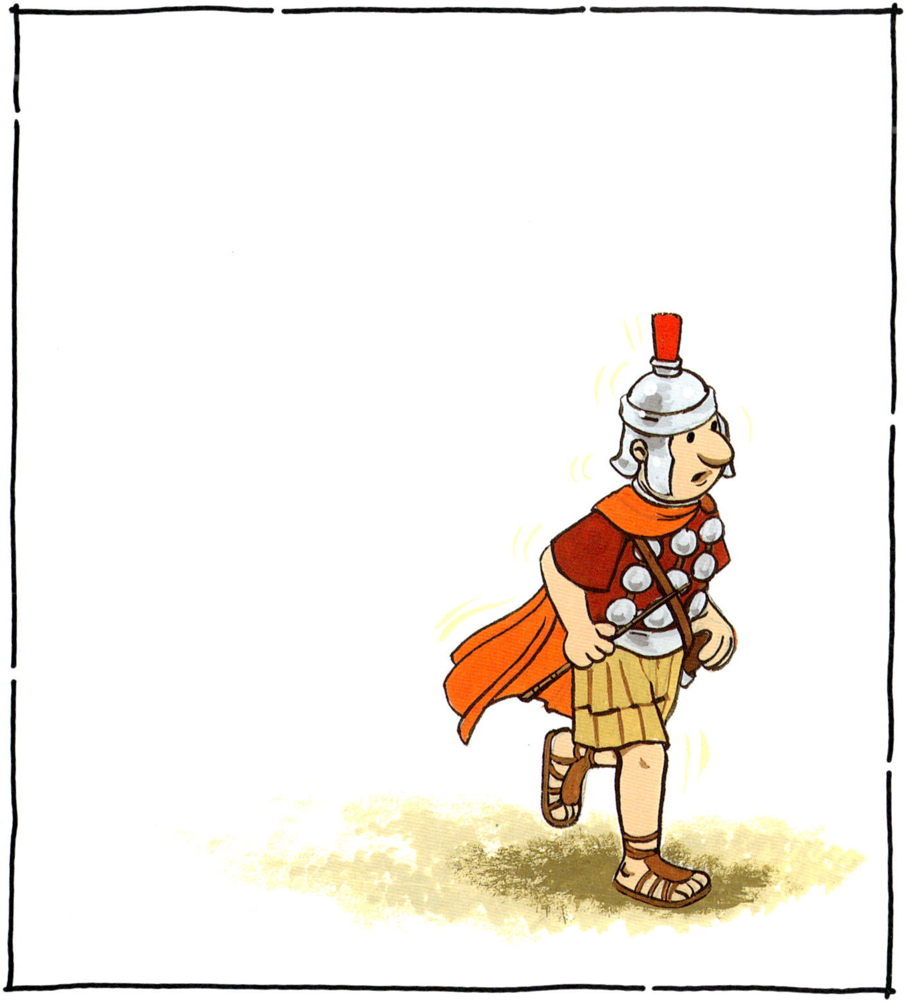

Just as he reached his doorway, Festin was bounding out, so they ran into each other, laughing and whooping with joy. For Festin was just as strong and just as bouncy as he had always been. His illness had vanished.

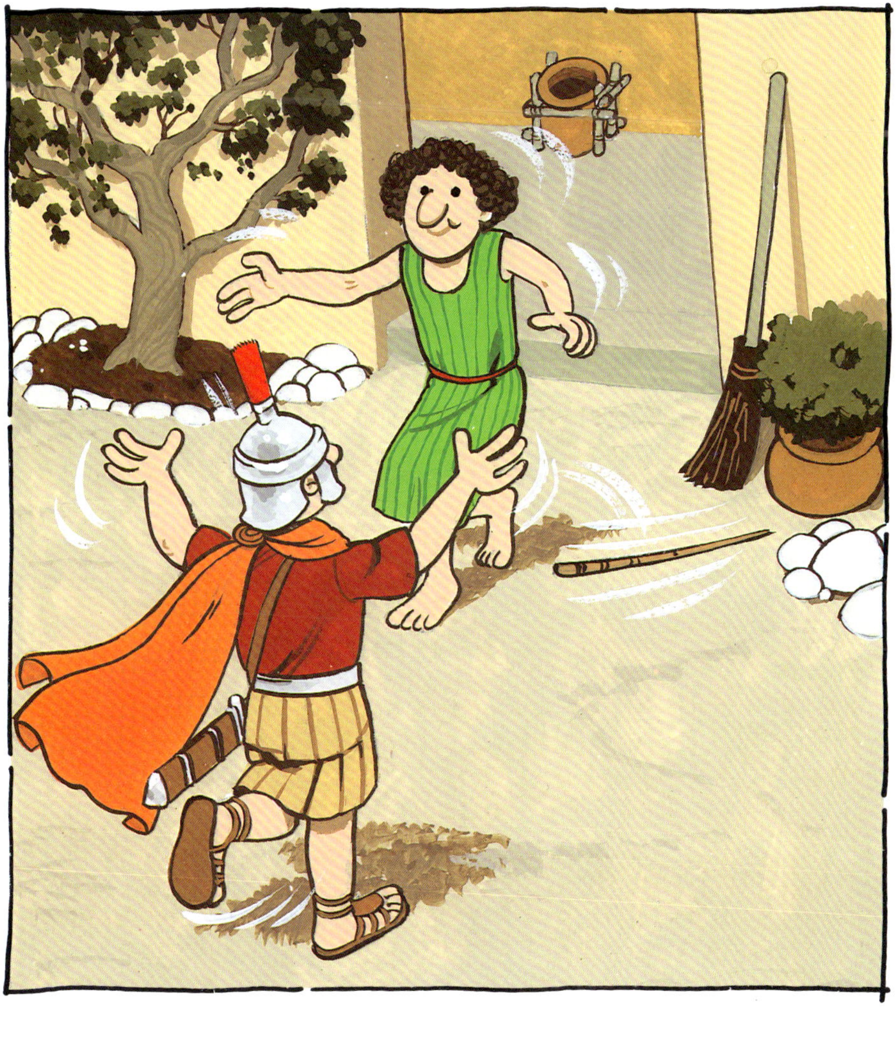

Quentus lifted him high on his shoulders so he could see Jesus. 'There is the man who made you better, Festin,' said Quentus, gently.

'I trusted him to heal you and he didn't let me down.' So together they walked to Jesus, to thank him.

A note for parents:
This story can be found in the Gospels according to Matthew, chapter 8, verses 5-13 and Luke, chapter 7, verses 1-10.